Water Culture

TROLLEY

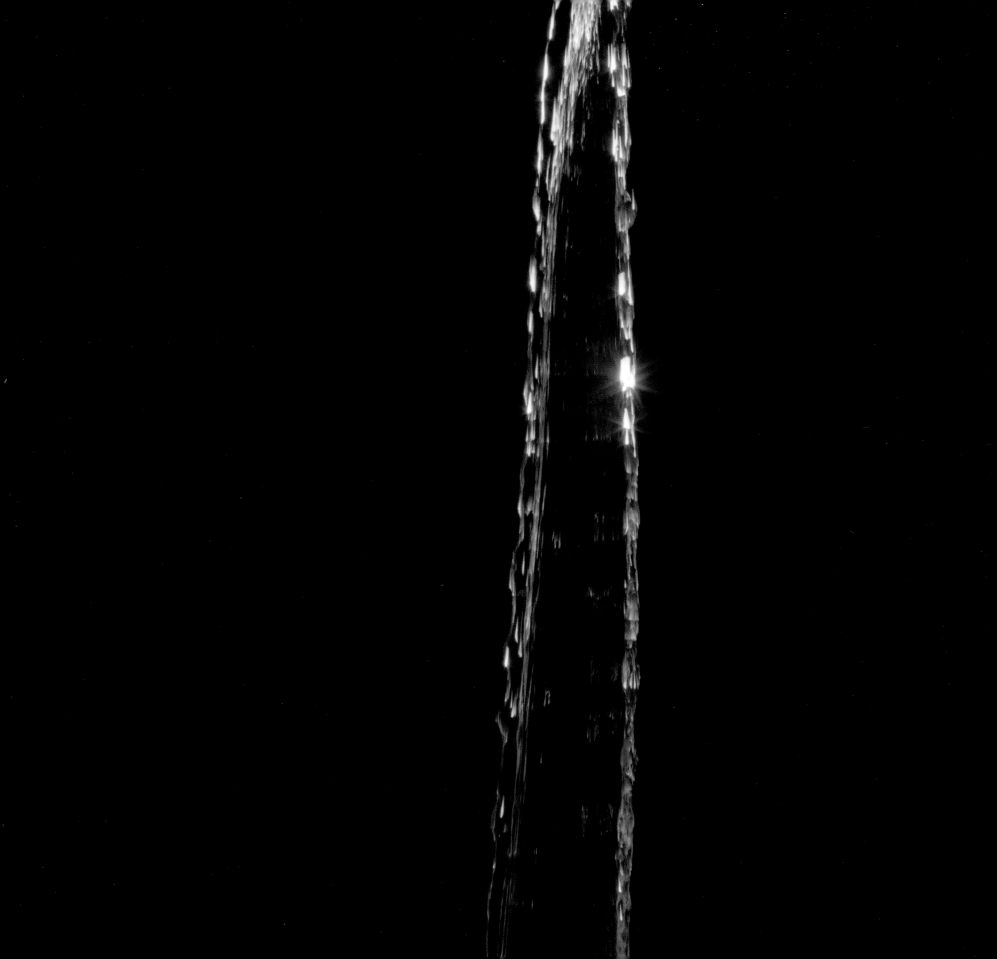

OVER TWO-THIRDS OF THE EARTH'S FRESH WATER
EXISTS AS ICE IN THE FORM OF GLACIERS AND ICE CAPS

JEAN-MICHEL COUSTEAU

PRESIDENT, OCEAN FUTURES SOCIETY

Q: How does it feel when you are in this whole other world that exists underwater?

A: I'm able to disconnect from the pettiness of everyday life. Underwater, I can fly like a bird, swim like a fish. The serenity there allows me to completely rejuvenate myself, recharge my batteries, and be utterly fulfilled. Under water I begin to understand how complex and extremely well organized nature is and realize that man is an intricate part of it.

Q: What is the most important thing you think the world should know about water?

A: Life has been around for billions of years; man, just a few million, a fraction of that time; and we may disappear in another fraction. We need to rediscover our connection to nature and the fact that our lives completely depend upon it. As a species we're ill equipped and almost didn't make it: we have no claws or fangs, and we had to steal skins from dead animals and hide in caves. Thanks to our minds, hands, and tools, we've come out of the caves in record time. But in the process, we've disconnected ourselves from an environment that supports us, and we have jeopardized the fundamental elements of our survival—air and water.

Q: Are oil spills the biggest threat to our oceans and marine life, now that 6,000 petrol tankers roam the seas each day?

A: The biggest problem is that we use the ocean as a garbage can. As long as we continue to allow run-off and tankers to criss-cross the ocean full of oil and even more hazardous substances, like toxic waste and radioactive material, we will have problems.

The second biggest threat is the destruction of coastal habitats. Life exists everywhere in the ocean, but most of it is in the coastal zone, where man has had the biggest impact. In the name of economic progress, we continually remove and destroy dunes, marshlands and reefs, wiping out reproduction, predation, and proper nesting grounds. No hotel or parking lot is worth the elimination of a species.

The third problem is the fact that we can't manage the planet; only pieces of it. Fishing is anarchy, and every man is for himself, except in economic zones where we try to enforce regulations. This works fine for rich nations, but the majority of the world can't enforce these laws. And it's become a catastrophe. The 93 species of ocean life that we normally depend on are overfished. I'm for the revolutionary concept of farming the ocean away from the ocean. We could open fish farms on land where the demand is, places like Kansas City and Baghdad. My vision is to farm fish or shrimp in giant indoor tanks, with big fish on upper levels and smaller ones on lower levels, and they all get served fresh at a street-level restaurant.

Q: Experts say that the surface temperature of the Earth is expected to increase by 1.4 to 5.8 degrees Celsius (34.5 °F - 42.4 °F) by 2100. What are the effects of this?

A: Ocean levels are rising, the ice caps are melting, and coastal erosion is taking place. One- to two-degree increases in temperature can kill whole coral reefs in just a few weeks.

Q: For you, what have been some of the most heartbreaking ecological disasters?

A: In Fiji, when gold is extracted from the land, chemicals like cyanide are used and the tailings—that is, the refuse remaining after ore has been processed—are supposed to be contained, but they are not. Although the country is required to practice environmental protection, gigantic amounts of toxic tailings have entered the rivers, and thousands of fish have died from chemical poisoning. The sediments from run-off choked the reefs to death and created a cloud that filtered out the sunlight, starving the plants and bleaching the coral. The Fiji gold mine went bankrupt, and the owners walked away, but rain continues to wash the poisonous tailings to the reef, and no one there is held accountable.

Then there are the oil spills from the *Exxon Valdez* and the *Prestige*. Aside from the obvious mass destruction of marine life, there was also the unbelievable long-term social, cultural, and psychological impact on humans. Families were broken up, economies destroyed, partnerships broken, drugs introduced, alcohol abused, and jails filled. Fortunately, new regulations in the U.S.A. have been passed to phase out single-hull tankers and create emergency response stations. In Europe, the *Prestige* disaster accelerated this process, and the European Parliament is phasing out single-hull tankers earlier than planned.

Perhaps catastrophes have finally triggered something positive, and we are finally beginning to learn through grief.

Q: What is your own commitment to turning the tide of water devastation?

A: By all possible means, we must connect the ocean to the existence of every human being. This is the only way for people to understand that the quality of each and every one of our lives depends on water, depends on the ocean. My father said, "People protect what they love," and so we want more people to fall in love with water. And Ocean Futures says, "Protect the ocean and you protect yourself." Kill the ocean, and you're committing suicide.

Q: In order to stay hopeful, what can we look towards?

A: Young people, young people, and more young people. They have nothing to lose and are investing in the long term. They're not in handcuffs like today's adults, crippled by the debts of a credit system that has us living beyond our means. We may fight for freedom, but we are slaves to our own lifestyles. Young people don't have these problems, and they are learning faster than we did and by our bad example. They also have access to information we didn't have.

And nongovernmental organisations (NGOs) are part of the solution. Governments are short-term by nature and must prove themselves quickly. Industries are worse because they have to make a profit immediately. NGOs are long-term, are not forced to make a profit, and can look ahead. They're the ones who can make the link with the future.

Q: What water issues come to mind that I may not have asked about?

A: To me, it's that a child under five years of age is going to die before I finish this sentence because of a lack of water. Forty-one thousand children die every day. That's the equivalent of seventy-eight 747s crashing daily, and it's not acceptable. It's repulsive. We have the ability to provide water to each of these children, but what we are lacking is the collective will to accomplish this. What are we waiting for? This is the commitment we need to make to the children of the world.

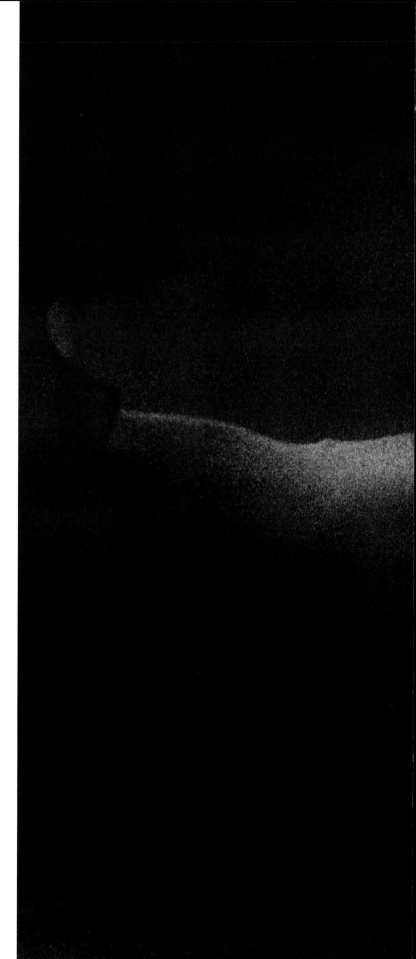

ONE OUT OF FIVE ADULT BELUGA WHALES IN THE
ST. LAWRENCE RIVER IN CANADA SUFFERS FROM
CANCER—THEIR BODIES ARE CONTAMINATED WITH
HIGH LEVELS OF INDUSTRIAL CONTAMINANTS

PRESIDENT MIKHAIL GORBACHEV
PRESIDENT, GREEN CROSS INTERNATIONAL

Q: What is the most dramatic example of the devastation of a body of water you have witnessed in your lifetime?

A: As secretary for agriculture of the Soviet Union from 1978 to 1985, I inherited the catastrophe of the destruction of the Aral Sea, arguably the most tragic example of the consequences of irresponsible human manipulation of watercourses. The two rivers that fed the Aral Sea had been diverted to irrigate cotton fields, leaving the sea to dry up and create a dust bowl, which has devastated health and livelihoods across the Central Asian region. The strangling of the Aral Sea showed how water touched every aspect of people's lives, from cooking, washing, and drinking to the cultural fabric of communities whose lives centred entirely on the sea. Decades later, and with the breakup of the Soviet Union, this environmental and humanitarian disaster is now shared by five newly independent states and Russia, adding the potential for interstate conflicts to the already overwhelming problems. This nightmare situation was one of the catalysts of my decision to dedicate myself to environmental protection and the struggle to change our system of values with respect to the planet.

Q: At this point in our human history, we know more and are richer than ever. Why then can't we solve the big problems of the planet, such as water pollution and the lack of safe drinking water?

A: It is true that we are now in the unique position of not only knowing the consequences of our abuse of the environment—although many continue to deny them—but also having the privilege of well-developed alternatives to our current destructive ways.

Unfortunately, many of the most powerful people in the world lack the courage to choose these alternatives. This is the essence of the problem: a lack of political courage. We have the money, science, and technology to provide clean drinking water to every human being on Earth, but this will not happen unless the leaders of developed countries and big business dedicate the necessary resources and the leaders of developing countries make it a priority.

Q: How can governments, industries, and people be persuaded to act more robustly for the well-being of our waters?

A: Politicians are concerned about security, the economy, and, ultimately, re-election. For water to be considered the priority issue that it clearly is, it is necessary to convince governments that it is a security issue and an economic issue. The benefits that accrue from efficient water management and distribution do indeed include regional stability and sustainable economic development; poor management and neglect have just the opposite effect. Green Cross International's Water for Peace program places water firmly in the security context and encourages the public participation, cooperation, and dialogue necessary for preventing conflicts. In addition, Green Cross is constantly calling for greater financial resources to be dedicated to water. It is now established that we need some $100 billion a year, in addition to current outlays, in order to reach the Millennium Goals of halving the proportion of people in the world without clean drinking water and basic sanitation. This finance must be found; there are no excuses for failing in this task.

Q: Is it feasible for warring neighbouring countries to cooperate on issues of vital importance, such as the flow of the Jordan River?

A: There is a reason why, since antiquity, it has been against the laws of war to poison your enemy's water. In general, transboundary waters are governed according to the national interests of the most powerful states in a basin, but, even amongst the most bitter adversaries there is a reluctance to completely deny water to a neighbor. During the first Gulf war, Turkey permitted the use of its airspace and military bases for the conflict but refused to cut off the supply of the Tigris and Euphrates rivers to downstream Iraq. India and Pakistan have been to war three times and on the brink of war almost constantly since their separation in 1947, but they have never fought over the use of the shared Indus River. And even during the most violent phases of the Israel–Palestine conflict, the water authorities and experts from both sides have met regularly to keep the water supply in order. That said, water is a highly political and strategic issue, and it would be naïve not to realize that states think foremost of their own interests and that conflicts and even wars can be ignited over fierce competition for shared resources.

Q: In view of the many tragedies you have personally witnessed throughout your life, do you still believe that human beings can make things right?

A: Absolutely. Everybody of my generation has been touched by the many miseries of the 20th century, but despite everything, I remain an optimist and believe that it is possible to be both an optimist and a realist. It is still not too late to save the planet and ourselves. All around the world there are inspiring examples of communities and individuals making a difference, and there is a growing community of experts, activists, and leaders who are turning things in the right direction. As president of Green Cross, I have been privileged to meet people from every continent who work to improve their own communities' welfare through preserving the environment. This public awareness and motivation is growing, and ultimately it is this that will create the momentum for real change in our behaviour and lead to more responsible decision-making by politicians.

Q: Is there anything else you would like to talk about that we haven't touched upon already?

A: Well, I have learnt that water moves people. More than any other resource, even those as precious as oil and diamonds, water defines nations and inspires people. It is intricately entwined in our religions, cultures, and histories. Rivers were the original pathways and centres for the growth of human civilizations across the world, whether on the banks of the Euphrates, the Yangtze, or the Amazon, and for the transfer of people, goods, and ideas. These rivers have sustained life for millennia, but in the short space of time since we have gained the technology to do so, we have thoughtlessly tampered with, dammed, and contaminated them. We can never have the Aral Sea back as it was—it is lost forever. The same applies to the formerly vast marshlands of Mesopotamia and the estuary of the Colorado River. This is a violation of our past and future, and we need a new model of development that respects nature, cultures, and the needs of all.

THE ARAL SEA IN RUSSIA IS NOW A DEAD SEA
IN TURN AGRICULTURAL LIVELIHOODS AND FISHERIES
ARE COLLAPSING, AND LARGE AREAS HAVE TURNED INTO
PESTICIDE-LADEN DUST THAT
IS BLOWING OVER LOCAL INHABITANTS

NITRATE EXTRACTION FROM THE SOIL CREATES POLLUTION
THROUGH MINING CHEMICALS AND MACHINERY
AND DUMPING OF SOIL IN LOCAL WATERS.
CHILE IS THE LARGEST LEADING PRODUCER OF NITRATES

APPROXIMATELY 10 LITERS OF WATER ARE REQUIRED
TO MANUFACTURE ONE LITER OF GASOLINE

ONE LITER OF OIL CAN CONTAMINATE ONE MILLION LITERS OF WATER

APPROXIMATELY 300,000 WHALES, DOLPHINS, AND PORPOISES ARE ACCIDENTALLY CAUGHT AND DIE EACH YEAR IN FISHING NETS

CAROL BELLAMY
EXECUTIVE DIRECTOR, UNITED NATIONS CHILDREN'S FUND

Q: What is the situation of safe drinking water for children worldwide?

A: In 2000, some 1.1 billion people—about one-sixth of the world's population—still lacked access to safe drinking water. The majority live in Asia and Africa. In Sub-Saharan Africa, for example, two out of five people do not have access to improved water sources.

The situation for sanitation is even worse. About 2.4 billion people—80% of them in Asia—still lacked access to improved sanitation in the year 2000.

Water- and sanitation-related disease, although largely preventable, remains one of the most significant health problems worldwide. Mortality from diarrhoeal disease for children under five declined from 4.6 million in 1982 to 2.1 million in 2001, but the overall health burden of morbidity has not decreased. Millions of children are malnourished, physically stunted, and mentally retarded or blind, as a result of water- and sanitation-related disease and infections.

Q: Every 24 seconds 100 babies are born around the world. Almost 20 of them will not have access to clean drinking water. What is it like for a child born in these water-deprived conditions?

A: Such a child faces great challenges right from the start, since water is an essential element for a healthy, nurturing environment. Access to a clean water supply and sanitation is vital to a child's survival, development, and well-being.

About 4 billion cases of diarrhoea per year cause 2.1 million deaths, mostly among children under five. A high burden of disease, from cholera, intestinal worms, trachoma, and schistosomiasis, results from poor sanitation, unsafe water, and unhygienic environments.

Healthy children need sufficient quantities of safe water for drinking, cooking, and washing. When clean water is available close to the home, children do not have to walk long distances each day to collect water, which means that they can attend school. This particularly affects girls, who are usually allocated the chore of collecting water.

Q: Has the world community made any progress in the past 30 years regarding this situation?

A: During the period 1990–2000, global access to water supply rose by 5%, from 77% to 82%. This means that nearly 1 billion people gained access to improved water sources over the decade. The greatest gain in improved water coverage was registered in South Central Asia (from 72% to 85%). The lowest coverage rates remain in Sub-Saharan Africa, where only 58% of the population have access.

Over the same period, access to improved sanitation increased by 10% to 61% globally. Despite these gains, in 2000 about 2.4 billion people, 80% of them in Asia, still lacked access.

Q: Why is it that some people and governments still do not take the issue of water and sanitation seriously?

A: Even in countries where access to improved drinking water is good, poor water resources management practices and inadequate environmental sanitation are constraints to health and improved livelihoods. The ever-increasing competition for water affects the poor the most, especially women and girls, who have the burden of providing for minimal household needs. Water scarcity causes conflict within households, among communities, and between countries. Inadequate management and control of hazardous wastes and lack of awareness on how to mitigate naturally occurring contaminants in water (such as arsenic, nitrates, and fluoride) have directly affected children's environmental health, especially among poor children.

Q: How can poor countries achieve well-being for their populations when water is scarce or contaminated?

A: One of the best interventions that poor countries can promote is the simple practice of hand washing, which helps to block hand-to-mouth disease transmission. This can be done most effectively within school-based programmes, which ensure that access to water and sanitation facilities are reinforced with hygiene education.

There are many low-cost ways to improve the quality of water, including solar water purification and simple water filtering. Such small-scale interventions designed, planned, and implemented with community involvement can have an immediate effect in reducing the incidence of diarrhoea and other water-related infections.

Q: You meet children all over the world on a weekly basis. What are the most poignant things they say about water or ask you for?

A: Young people from all regions of the world have joined UNICEF discussion boards and participated in such events as the Children's World Water Forum, held in Japan in March 2003, to explore the importance of water, environment, and sanitation for their daily lives—and for their future. The variety and complexity of the issues that are addressed clearly demonstrate young people's belief that water is key to development and progress. Young people feel very strongly that water is not only a basic need but a basic right that is required for our survival and must be conserved. Some of their comments explore these issues:

"Lack of access to clean water is a problem today for some of our communities, especially in Africa. Don't they know that this is due to poverty and to alleviate this we'll need money and love…" (boy, 19, Cameroon)

"Here in Indonesia all water are already polluted. Not only in the big city like Jakarta, even in the small village like in Sukabumi… the problem not only the water but the most important thing that because more than 70% people in my country come from poor family, so they don't have a knowledge about clean water for themselves." (girl, 21, Indonesia)

"I guess governments in developing countries are not sensitive to the people's needs—everything is done to help the country develop economically, but at the expense of the welfare of the people. I think that the ultimate solution is for a more sensitive and selfless government; one that has a heart." (boy, 16, Singapore)

One of the greatest aspects I have seen in our children is the sense of optimism, and the dedication and belief that we can and must overcome this global problem: *"By joining forces, they will coalate our energy to create the strong synergy needed to avert a disaster that is threatening to become even worse."* (boy, 15, Kenya)

Q: What is your own commitment to ensuring that every child on Earth has access to clean water?

A: UNICEF believes that a safe water supply and sanitation are not only fundamental needs but a human right. UNICEF supports water, environment, and sanitation programmes in about 80 countries with a staff of over 180 professionals, both national and international. The decentralized nature of UNICEF operations allows it to assist governments and NGOs with innovative projects designed for local conditions. The organization's intersectoral involvement in promoting the well-being of children and women makes it possible for UNICEF to raise policy and strategy issues at the highest levels of government and at the same time to work with communities to address their particular needs.

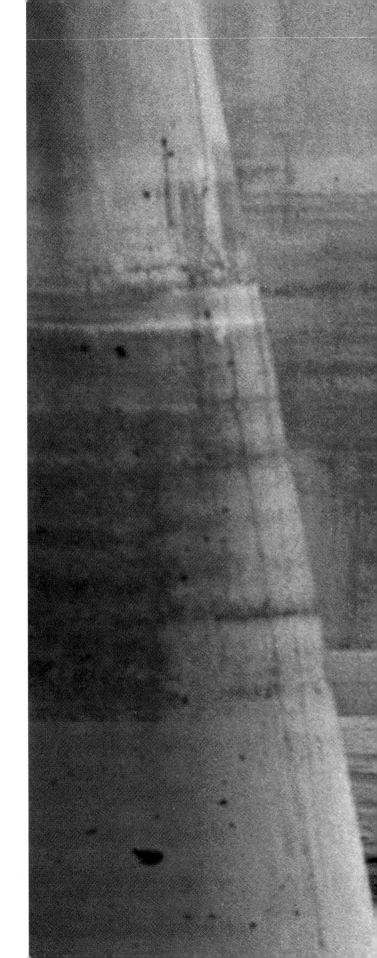

EVERY 24 SECONDS, 100 BABIES ARE BORN AROUND THE WORLD—
20 OF THEM WILL NOT HAVE ACCESS TO CLEAN DRINKING WATER

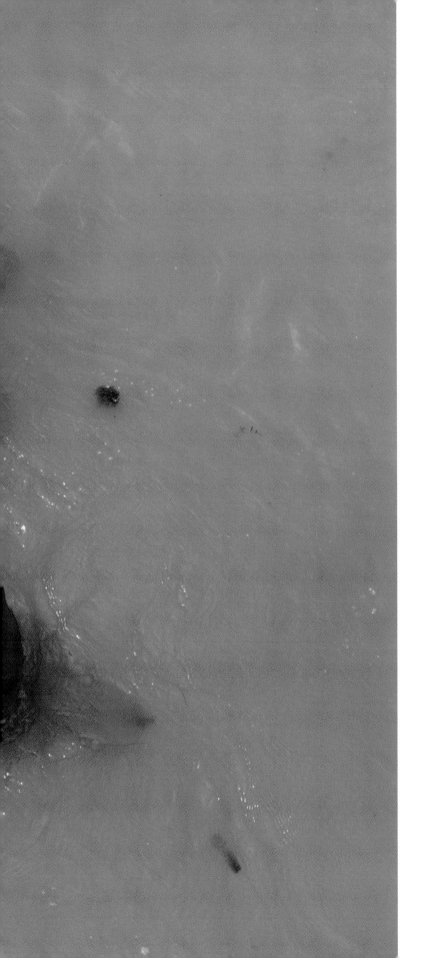

OF THE WORLD'S 500 MAJOR RIVERS,
MORE THAN HALF ARE SERIOUSLY POLLUTED
AND DEPLETED FROM OVER-USE

ROBERT F. KENNEDY, JR.

PRESIDENT, WATERKEEPER ALLIANCE

Q: What is the most important thing people should know about the state of water bodies in the United States and around the world?

A: In my work, the greatest thing we stress is that the public owns the waterways. This is true under most constitutional systems in the world. The waterways are not owned by the government or by corporations; they are public-trust assets owned by the people. Everybody has a right to use them, but nobody has a right to use them in a way that will diminish or injure their worth and enjoyment for others. Are we going to allow a few large corporations to dominate those public assets? Or are we going to keep those resources in the hands of the people?

In ancient Rome under the Justinian Code (one of the first written constitutions), assets that were not susceptible to private ownership were owned by the people. These included air, running waters, fisheries, wandering animals, wetlands, aquifers, and certain public lands. During the Dark Ages, when Roman law collapsed in Europe, the feudal lords and kings began trying to privatize the commons. For example, in England, King John erected navigational tolls on the Thames and sold monopolies of the fisheries to private parties. The public rose up to confront him on the fields of Runnymede, forcing him to sign the Magna Carta, which was the beginning of constitutional democracy. Most of the environmental rights are recognized in some form in almost every nation and culture around the world.

While the laws and constitution of every state in the U.S.A. stipulate that the fisheries and the waters of each state are owned by the people, the government and industry are constantly trying to act to privatize those waterways. For example, 30 years ago the state of New York gave permits to the General Electric Corporation to dump toxic PCBs into the Hudson River. Today, all the fish in the Hudson are too toxic to eat. GE got away with something that King John could not get away with: it transferred a public resource into a private one to make a profit. There was no due process, and the people who relied on those fisheries for recreation and their livelihood are now out of business. Their interests have been compromised because of the power and political clout of a large corporation. And this is happening all over the world where governments are increasingly allowing public trust assets—our public waterways—to be privatized. That is going to be the big battle of the 21st century. And already we are seeing violence in many nations, such as Bolivia, Mexico, and Belize, where large international corporations like Bechtel and Fortis make secret deals with government officials, allowing them to own the waterways of those nations. It is a real threat, not only to the environment but to our democracy.

Q: There are some rivers, such as the Hudson River in New York State, that were once sewers but were nurtured back to health. How was this accomplished?

A: Well, it happened after Earth Day 1970. At that time, our waterways in the U.S.A. were in terrible trouble: the Cuyahoga River burned for a week with flames that were eight stories high because of industrial pollution, the beaches in Southern California were closed for months as a result of the Santa Barbara oil spill in 1969, and Lake Erie was declared dead. Back then, 80% of the raw sewage in our country was being dumped into the waterways.

But on Earth Day 1970, the public rose up. Twenty million Americans—10% of the population—took to the streets, demanding that politicians return the ancient environmental rights to the people. It was the largest public demonstration in our history. The political system responded and began investing in our environmental infrastructure: 28 major environmental laws were passed in the next 10 years, including the Clean Water Act, and billions of dollars were spent building sewage treatment plants nationwide. Additionally, the public was given the right to have permit hearings, sue polluters, and participate in the dialogue over the destiny of those water systems. That is how the waters in the U.S.A. were restored: through citizen participation and public moneys allocated by Congress.

Q: Are farms the single biggest source of water contamination in the U.S.A.?

A: Farm practices in the U.S.A. are responsible for only a fraction of the pollution. But it is a large fraction and one that is growing because of new industrialized farm practices that have displaced traditional ones. For example, with pork production, farmers shoehorn up to 100,000 animals into tiny cages. A hog produces ten times more waste than a human being, so a facility with 100,000 animals will produce more waste than a city of 1 million people. That waste is dumped onto fields and eventually reaches the waterways, contaminating the water. This is happening all over the U.S.A.

Q: What is the biggest source of pollution to our urban drinking water?

A: Paved surfaces are the biggest threat to our waterways today; more so than industrial farming. Pavement transports pollution very efficiently. When it rains, pesticides, fertilizer, trash, automobile fluids, and other toxic substances deposited on the streets, parking lots, construction sites, and industrial facilities flow directly into our waterways. Unwise development—instances where we are paving over the farm landscapes—is a much larger source of pollution than the large-scale farms. For instance, the greatest threat to New York City's water supply today is the suburbanization of upstate communities.

We recently signed an agreement that requires New York City to spend $1.5 billion in the upstate communities, ensuring their economic vitality and rebuilding their environmental infrastructures. In exchange for that investment, the upstate communities have agreed to limit development in their open spaces to allow the towns and cities to grow upwards but not to spread outwards onto the landscapes.

Q: How can the readers of this book stay hopeful that we will be able to make things right by water?

A: The most important thing is for people to join an environmental-advocacy group that fights for their rights to clean water. There is no guarantee that our water systems will be protected. Today, the threat to our water supplies, particularly from large corporations, is daunting. But it's like everything else in life: every individual has to do his best to make the world a better place, then leave the results to God. The forces that we are fighting are powerful, relentless, and merciless, and if we do not put all our energies into the fight, we are going to lose our water supplies.

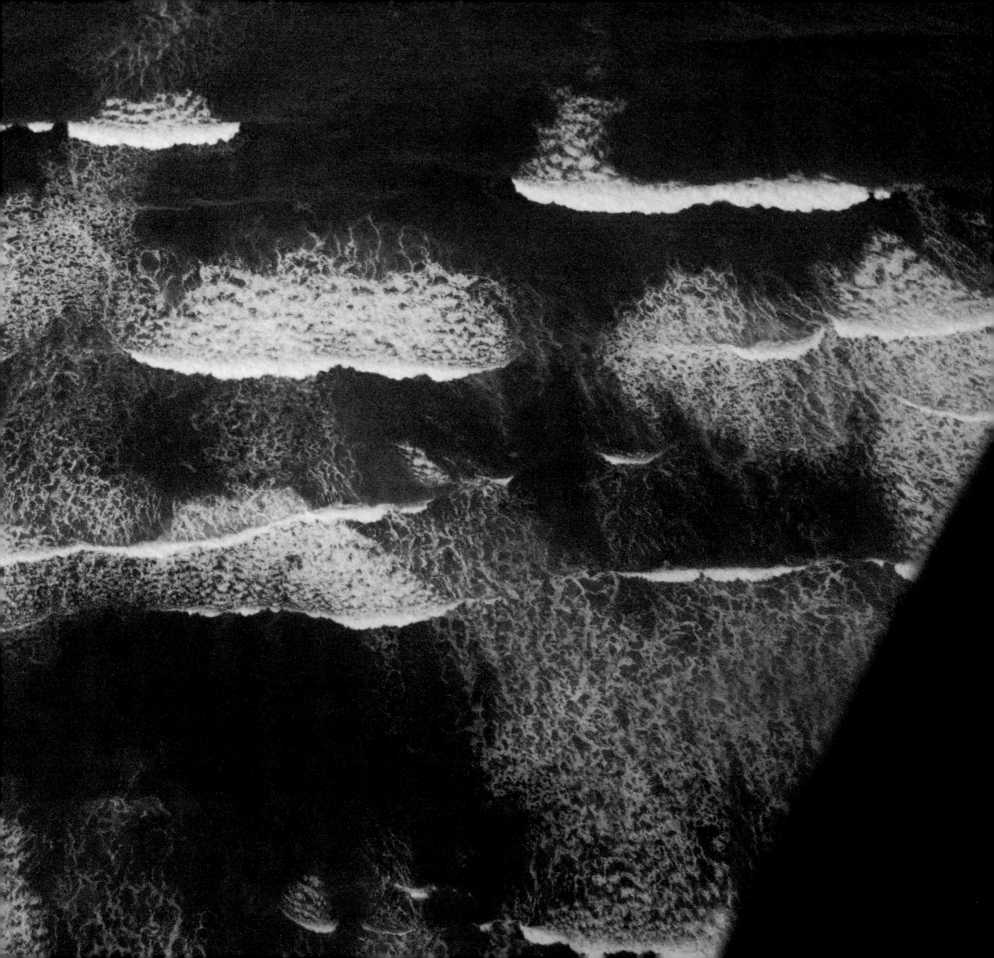

DR. MAHMOUD A. ABU-ZEID
PRESIDENT, WORLD WATER COUNCIL

Q: Are we in a water crisis today?

A: Indeed, we are facing many water crises. The 21st century is being heralded as the age of water scarcity. Global population is growing so fast that it has already passed the 6 billion mark, and water demands, which are rapidly increasing, exceed the limited water supply in many areas in the world. Only 82% of the world's population has access to a regular water supply, while just 60% has access to sanitation. Currently about 26 nations face a chronic water shortage, affecting their ability to meet their food needs and threatening the livelihood of their people. By the year 2025 this number is expected to have risen to include 66 countries.

Then there are the transboundary issues. With more than 260 transboundary rivers in the world, you have 260 potential sources of conflict, especially in the arid regions, where fierce competition for water resources will intensify in the future.

Also, an increase in industrialization, urbanization, and agrochemicals use has produced large volumes of effluent wastewater, which is often discharged into waterways that serve as sources of freshwater supplies to downstream communities. The resultant water-related diseases are responsible for the deaths of more than 6,000 people, most of them children, every day.

The water crisis is not just a matter of having too little water to satisfy our needs; it is also about managing water so badly that the environment and billions of people suffer.

Q: Are we currently using more water than is really necessary to sustain our human needs? Who takes advantage of water the most?

A.: Most of it is used in the agriculture sector, which consumes 80% of the global water budget. Yet water use efficiency in that realm is only 45%. In other words, we are losing more than half of an already limited water budget. Gross offences against water savings include huge losses at the tail ends of canals, leakage in the distribution systems, and incorrect placement of dams, creating excess evaporation. An improvement of just 10% in the efficiency of irrigation could conserve enough water to double the global amount available for drinking. Food security for 8 billion people would require a 15% to 20% increase in water supply and a 30% increase in cultivated areas by the year 2025.

Q: What is the role of privately owned enterprises in water issues?

A: Water is not an owned commodity in most of the world and is generally considered a "public good." Nevertheless, recognition is rapidly growing that the main road to improving the efficiency of water resource management would involve the participation of the private sector. It could also go beyond the public sector's ability in filling the financial gap. But it is equally accepted that ownership of the resource and of many of the infrastructure assets is best left with the public sector.

Q: It is estimated that some 3 billion people will face water scarcity by 2025. If we really wanted to, could we ensure that all people on Earth have access to water for their vital needs?

A: We could, but of course, much needs to be done. The United Nations Millennium Development Goals call for halving the proportion of people without access to safe drinking water and sanitation by the year 2015. To achieve our goals, we obviously need to massively increase investments in water, but we also have to build better-capacity storage, establish good governance, secure the cooperation and adoption of integrated water resource management, involve all stakeholders in integrated management, increase public funding for research and innovation in the public interest, link monitoring activities, and strengthen the role of the private sector.

Q: What is the most inspiring possibility or idea you know of that can make us believe in a bright blue future for the planet?

A: This is very difficult question. Working hard could help us to achieve a lot. Patience could help to harvest what we have grown. We are facing seven challenges in the water crisis: water scarcity, lack of access, deterioration of quality, uncertain peace and security, lack of awareness by decision-makers and the public, decline of financial resources, and fragmentation of water management processes.

The World Water Vision was prepared after the second World Water Forum and presents what many believe are realistically achievable goals over the next 25 years. At the third World Water Forum, in 2003, we called upon the governments of the world to shoulder the responsibility for action on the ground, giving more responsibility and authority to local governments and communities.

Q: Floods are the most damaging of all natural disasters, and the number of victims and economic losses increases every year. Can we expect water-related tragedies to multiply?

A: Every year, floods are responsible for the homelessness and deaths of millions and for billions of dollars in material damages. Additional suffering is inflicted through the spreading of such conditions as diarrhoea and malaria.

Floods occur all over the world, even in arid regions, and recent studies report that floods are becoming more frequent. Unfortunately, floods are also unpredictable. Luckily, forecasting methods and designs for protection are improving, so we expect less damage in the future. Building capacity is very important in reducing flood disasters, especially for women. At the third World Water Forum, in 2003, the question was clearly posed: When floods strike, who is usually at home to face the crisis?

Q: Is there anything else you would like to share with us?

A: People between the ages of 20 and 29 represent 16.6% of the entire world population. This particular age group should be a focus for our efforts because of the massive energy it can put into driving sustainable development in general and the water sector in particular. If properly organized, a youth movement could influence global water resources policy-making and transform vision into action.

IN THE U.S.A., IT IS ESTIMATED THAT THE AMOUNT OF OIL RUN-OFF
FLOWING FROM URBAN PAVEMENTS AND INTO THE OCEANS CREATES
THE EQUIVALENT OF AN *EXXON VALDEZ* OIL SPILL EVERY 8 MONTHS

WETLANDS ACT AS FILTERS BY INTERCEPTING SURFACE RUN-OFF
AND POLLUTANTS, PROCESSING ORGANIC WASTES, AND CONTROLLING FLOODS

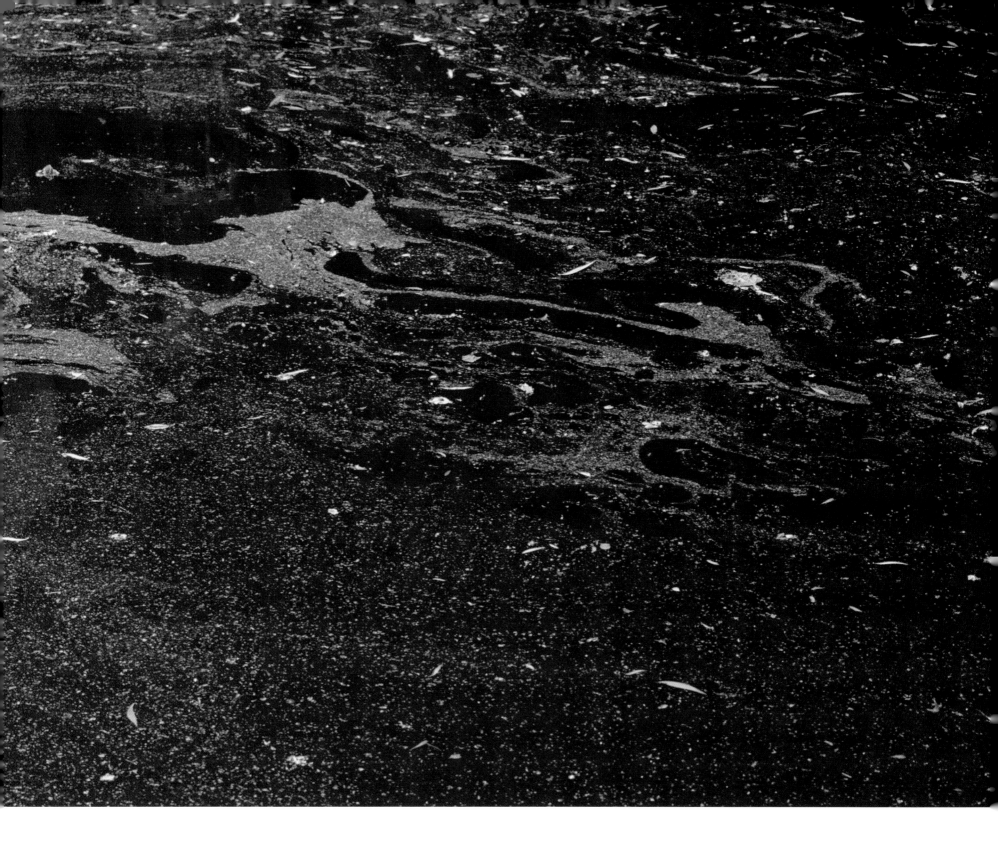

MORE THAN ONE BILLION PEOPLE LACK ACCESS
TO AN IMPROVED WATER SUPPLY AND 2.4 BILLION
TO IMPROVED SANITATION

RYAN HRELJAC
FOUNDER, RYAN'S WELL FOUNDATION

Q: What was it like when you drank water from the first well that your pocket money helped to build in Uganda when you were just six years old?

A: I can't even tell you what a great feeling it was! It made me think that I did something right. It's just one small step to making the world a better place.

Q: How much does it cost to build a well in an African village?

A: The cost to build a well depends on the country. A well in Ethiopia costs more (about $15,000) because of the mountains and because it takes more for the workers to drill down to the water table. In Uganda it costs about $2,000.

Q: How many wells have you so far built in Africa? How do you do it? And how old are you now?

A: We have stopped keeping track of the exact number of wells that are in Africa now. But I know it's more than 70. We learned that we have to raise money for a well but also for many other things to do the whole project. We need money to train the people who are helping to build and fix the wells, for transportation, for latrines, and for places for people to wash their hands, too. I have learned that by washing your hands after you go to the toilet or before you are cooking food, you can cut down on illnesses by one-third. Now we are raising money for the whole project, and that means water and sanitation.

I saved on my own at the start when I was six years old, but with lots and lots of help from other people and from the Canadian International Development Agency (CIDA), we have helped raise over $750,000. There is even a foundation now called the Ryan's Well Foundation. Teachers and other volunteers are helping me to spread the word about how children can help adults make a difference, whether it's helping with clean water or helping with something else.

I am now 12 years old.

Q: Why don't people take dirty water and boil it to make it clean?

A: In Uganda and in other countries in Africa, people have to search for miles and miles to get enough firewood for their families. There isn't a lot around. People in Africa don't have enough wood to boil the water they need every day. In Africa some people are starting to plant more trees so that there will be more forests and more wood in the future, but right now there is a problem because there isn't enough wood. Everything is connected!

Q: What is your dearest water dream?

A: I dream of the day when everyone in the world has clean water. That's a big dream. I learned, though, that you can do anything, but only if you really try hard and you really want to.

I found out where my puzzle piece fits in the world, and that is with water. I just hope everyone else finds out where their puzzle piece fits, too. Who knows? If all the kids and adults work together and they never give up, then maybe someday there will be peace and clean water for everyone on Earth.

Q: What is it like for you to see the misery of other children who don't have it as good as you do?

A: At my new drilling rig in Uganda, I met two boys who were very nice, but meeting them made me very sad. Their stomachs were all sticking out. They were sick from drinking dirty water. That made me feel sick too. From my bedroom, I take seven steps and I have it—clean water right at my tap! In Africa, so many kids have to walk for hours and hours just to get a drink. I am so lucky because I live in a country that has lots of clean water, but kids in other countries are not as lucky. Some kids spend many hours during the day fetching water for their families, so they cannot go to school. That's just not fair. No one should have to live like that.

Q: You have attended conferences all over the world. What is the most important thing you tell adults?

A: I tell them to please remember not to waste water. I tell them to turn off the tap straight away when they brush their teeth or have a shower. And I tell them not to pollute the water in our rivers and oceans. I heard that someday more of us might run out of fresh clean water. If we are not careful, one day when you want a drink, maybe it will be gone so we have to take care of the water we drink and we have to learn to share our water with everybody, or we're all going to be in big trouble.

People ask me if I'm sad because my friends in Africa are poor. They want to know if I am sad because I live in a brick house and they live in mud and grass houses. They might be poor because they don't have much money, but in other ways they are not poor at all.

I have learned a lot in the past five years, especially from people who live in Africa. I've learned how important water is. Water is life. There are amazing adults like Nelson Mandela doing great things to make the world a better place. He is like a big old oak tree, and kids like us are like little seedlings. But with lots of water, sun, and love, maybe we will grow up to be big old oak trees too.

Whether you are the prime minister of Canada, the president of the United States, a gas station clerk, or a kid in grade seven like me, you can make a difference in the world, but only if you really try hard and really want to. Just pick a dream and then go for it. Oh, and never give up!

DR. PETER H. GLEICK

PRESIDENT, THE PACIFIC INSTITUTE

Q: As one of the leading authoritative figures on global freshwater systems, what is the most compelling argument you can make to persuade us to act for the cause of our planet's waters?

A: We have entered the 21st century dreaming of a technological and communications revolution, yet billions of people still lack the most basic water services: clean drinking water and adequate sanitation. At the same time, our water policies have led to the destruction of aquatic ecosystems around the world. It is also increasingly clear that global climate changes are coming and that they will have significant effects on our water resources—yet we have barely begun to think about this problem and to act to address it. We must act now to move to a more sustainable vision of water for all.

Q: Can we afford to manage our planet's freshwater in a sustainable manner?

A: Frankly, the costs to us of doing the right thing are far less than the cost of failing to manage our water in a sustainable manner. These costs of not managing our water properly include water-related deaths and illnesses, lost educational opportunities for children who become sick, growing conflicts over shared water resources, and unavoidable climate changes affecting water availability and quality and triggering disasters. If we don't move toward sustainable water management now, the costs to society will be high. Yet far too few resources are devoted to this problem. Despite the vast needs, international funding for water is declining, not growing.

Q: Some 260 rivers in the world flow through more than one country. Are water conflicts on the rise, and will they be a truly significant issue to contend with in the future?

A: Conflicts over shared water resources appear to be increasing in scope and magnitude, both between nations and within nations—conflicts between farms and cities. In just the past few years we've seen growing disputes in the Middle East, southern Asia, and even North America. Most of these lead not to violence but to negotiation and cooperation, but far greater efforts are needed to reduce the risks of water-related violence. Of special concern are the shared waters of the Tigris, Euphrates, Jordan, and Nile rivers in the Middle East and of the great rivers of Asia flowing through large population centers and across borders of nations with conflicting political agendas.

Q: Should a vital resource such as water be considered an economic good, wherein it is priced, traded, and sold on the market by private companies?

A: Water is an economic good, but it is also a public good. In recent years, multinational water companies have begun to move into markets previously served (often inadequately, one must admit) by the public sector. These efforts at privatization have become highly controversial, as people have become concerned about protecting the public interest. A far better balance is needed: we must learn how to apply appropriate economic tools to help us manage water efficiently and effectively, but we must also learn how to protect the public interest where economics fails. Water is too important to be left solely in private hands.

Q: What is the most frightening thing that is going on in terms of water on Earth at present?

A: The failure to provide basic clean water for billions of people leads to between 2 and 5 million deaths every year from preventable water-related diseases. This is a scandal and should be unacceptable to governments and populations everywhere. I also worry about our seeming inability to understand the importance of basic water requirements for our natural ecosystems and the devastating consequences when we deprive them of these requirements.

Q: What makes you hopeful that we will be able to pull our "water survival" off?

A: A "soft path" for water is possible, integrating smart technology, appropriate economics, community decision making, efficient water use, and ecological thinking. We are moving off the hard path of relying solely on large infrastructure such as dams, reservoirs, and aqueducts to meet our needs. Such "hard" solutions have brought many benefits but many unexpected costs as well—economic, environmental, and social costs. I am optimistic that we are now beginning to move in a different direction, down the soft path. In the industrialized nations, demand for water is leveling off—even declining—as we learn how to meet our needs with less water and as we implement more efficient technologies and policies.

Q: What is the most detrimental water behavior we perpetrate in our homes? What can every single one of us do to contribute and help make things better?

A: The old adage goes, "Waste not, want not." We must rethink our water use in every sector of society. Each of our actions affects water quality and availability. By making smart water use central to our day-to-day actions, we can make a difference in each of our communities.

Q: What is the single most interesting thing you have ever found through your research and that most of us do not even suspect?

A: The potential to use water more efficiently and productively is vast and largely misunderstood. Our ultimate goal is to provide goods and services for society. If we can supply our needs and wants with less water, there will be more opportunities for meeting basic needs, for reducing conflicts over water allocation, and for restoring the natural ecosystems on which we all depend.

MARGARET CATLEY-CARLSON

CHAIR, THE GLOBAL WATER PARTNERSHIP

Q: Over one billion people have no access to running water, and women, who do the bulk of domestic work, suffer the most from this injustice. What do you feel when you look into the eyes of women afflicted by this kind of poverty?

A: I feel an acute sense of the waste of human potential. I imagine the time a woman will spend and the energy she will lose in fetching and carrying, the schooldays her daughters will miss when they must take over the task, and the heartbreak she will suffer when her children become ill or die unnecessarily as a result of waterborne diseases.

Q: Is there enough water on Earth to sustain the current population of 6 billion people, as well as our $43 trillion economy, both of which are growing?

A: It's going to be very difficult in some regions, particularly with the impact of climate change on already arid areas. The general consensus among water experts is that there IS enough water for all, provided we manage it differently and better. In most places, that translates into more public discussions about the allocation of available water, more responsibility by governments in their policy making and rule making and in their support of the science that propels change, and creative financing to create sustainable systems. We are talking about the ultimate public good. And public authorities must speak for and defend the segments within their governance that are voiceless—in this case, the poor and the environment.

Q: Is human greed the primary cause of water problems in the world?

A: Greed may be an unhelpful word. In many countries, more than 90% of the water is used for agriculture, often by large-scale farmers. However, they see themselves as essential food providers, employers, and income earners for their countries. Other industries also pollute, but they too provide jobs and foreign exchange, which are often in very short supply. The root cause of water problems is that too few people value water, and too few systems reward water-valuing behavior. We need to start building consensus in every area and region on how this can happen. Subsidy, law enforcement, and public campaigns may be part of the answer.

Q: In 2001 the size of the Aral Sea in Russia (once the fourth largest lake in the world) had decreased by 75%. What other water tragedies are currently playing out that need urgent attention?

A: Dozens of lakes in China have just disappeared, and the klongs in Bangkok are largely gone. In the 20th century humans destroyed 50% of available wetlands, while coral reefs everywhere are perilously threatened.

Q: The Colorado River, the Rio Grande, the Yellow River in China, the Indus, and many other of the world's largest rivers no longer reach the sea all year long. Why have these great bodies of water fallen silent?

A: Too often there are no controls on or barriers to upstream extraction, especially when it is fuelling economic development. As a result, the Syr Darya and Amu Darya no longer feed the Aral, and the Sind feels the pressure of saline intrusion. Some countries have enacted regulations, while billions of dollars have been poured into restoring Lake Biwa in Japan and the Murray Darling Basin in Australia; unfortunately, they are both years away from turnaround. But the Yalu River in China has reached the sea again for the past four years, as a result of deliberate policy enforcement.

Q: Does mobilizing money to finance the end of the water crisis take resources away from other vital programs? How much money is needed? Who should be paying?

A: About $180 billion is needed annually. That amount would help to store the water needed by people living with only periodic rainfall, provide and maintain systems for drinking-water delivery, install and care for sewers and sanitation, restore and improve irrigation systems, and protect water sources in general. This isn't all new—the world already spends about $70 billion each year. Most of the money comes from the budgets of the countries of the world. For new investment, the offshore donor or investor is a potential source; there has been a steady decline in such investment in the recent past.

Health, education, and infrastructure sectors all have financial needs, too. But there are alternatives for financing water. There are two sources for ongoing system costs: the taxpayer and the client. Cities of the developing world often have fragile or nonexistent tax bases. As a result, most cities let systems degrade, leakage in aqueduct infrastructures up to 40% or 50% is not uncommon, and irrigation systems lose water and use it inefficiently. The systems are kept functioning for the middle classes, but the poor are forced to buy more expensive water from vendors and private deliverers. We are all clients and have an interest in well-functioning systems. All should pay, most should pay more, and subsidies may well be needed for the poorest populations.

Q: What are the most important things a person reading this book can do to save our planet's waters?

A: Be aware. Value water. For example, take an intelligent interest in your own river basin—is it improving or degrading? Is there a basin authority? Can you go to meetings, or start one, or take part? How much of your basin pollution goes to the sea? Is there a plan to stop it?

Q: Is there proof that governments, businesses, banks, environmental groups, and academe can really work effectively together to solve the water crisis?

A: There are new and ingenious water laws all around the world. Water basin associations are coming into being. The new European Water Directive takes these issues very seriously. And as more and more countries experience water problems, interest grows in managing the resource of water. So far, we are better at talking about water problems and analysing them than at provoking real action, but the word is always the precursor to the deed.

Q: What is the most important thing we should all know about water?

A: It is essential to human life and all other life forms. The right to water, if not accompanied by an obligation to protect it and value it, will be a hollow promise.

NEARLY ONE BILLION PEOPLE DEPEND ON FISH
AS THEIR PRIMARY SOURCE OF PROTEIN, YET SOME
70% OF MARINE FISHERIES ARE OVER-EXPLOITED

THE WATER TABLE UNDER THE NORTH CHINA PLAIN,
WHICH PRODUCES 25% OF CHINA'S GRAIN HARVEST,
DROPS BY 1.5 METERS ANNUALLY

IN CANADA, ON AVERAGE 14% OF MUNICIPAL-PIPED WATER
IS LOST IN PIPELINE LEAKS—UP TO 40% TO 50%
IS LOST IN SOME DEVELOPING COUNTRY CITIES

STEVEN M. HILTON

PRESIDENT, CONRAD N. HILTON FOUNDATION

Q: You are an avid surfer. What place does water hold in your life?

A: Living near the ocean in Malibu, California, I'm fortunate to be able to enjoy surfing the waves. Surfing provides exercise, relaxation, camaraderie, fun, and a means of connecting with the beauty of God's wonderful creation—the ocean. On the water, I often see dolphins swimming close by, harbor seals chasing small fish, and pelicans gliding on the updraft from a cresting wave. Surfing is a rejuvenating experience; it makes me feel alive and linked to the world of water.

Q: Fish stocks are severely depleted worldwide. Does aquaculture (i.e., fish farming) offer a promising means of feeding the world?

A: Many experts believe that we are currently maximizing the catch of wild fish and shellfish, so aquaculture offers the potential to harvest more from the ocean. Aquaculture already provides a significant, and growing, percentage of the total salmon, shrimp, oyster, and seaweed production worldwide. In the United States, nearly all of the trout, catfish, crayfish, and oysters consumed are derived from fish farms. Although there are challenges with respect to ensuring that large fish farms do not create pollution or weaken wild stocks of fish, it appears that fish farming offers a viable way to increase food production for an expanding world population.

Q: Some 300 million to 500 million tons of heavy metals, solvents, toxic sludge, and other wastes accumulate each year in the world (in water, soil, air, and so on). What are the most powerful tools to persuade corporate leaders around the world to take resolute action for the protection of our blue planet?

A: In most cases, consumers are not aware of the environmental "costs" of certain goods and industries. The first step is to accurately identify point sources of pollution and then, through watchdog and advocacy efforts, communicate these findings to governmental agencies with oversight of such industries. Oversight agencies should require, within regulatory guidelines, companies that are polluting to clean up their act or suffer large penalty fines. The prospect of incurring penalties will motivate companies to incorporate processes that minimize the pollution created by their activities.

In addition to stronger regulatory controls, another, more positive tool for convincing corporate leaders of the importance of environmentally friendly practices is the providing of concrete examples of how businesses can save money by adopting conservation practices. This win-win approach is a powerful incentive for any business concerned with its bottom-line profitability.

Q: The United States withdraws about 341 billion gallons of freshwater each day. How can our water-craving societies alter our relationship to water?

A: In the United States, agriculture is the largest user of freshwater. Currently, the U.S. government provides significant subsidies to farmers growing crops, such as cotton, that require a great deal of water. If these subsidies are reduced or eliminated, there will be less incentive for farmers to plant cotton, and the result will be less demand for water.

Q: Worldwide, over 500 million people are at risk of becoming blind from trachoma disease, a condition caused by limited access to adequate water and sanitation. Are we making any progress?

A: Yes, control and elimination of blinding trachoma is showing encouraging progress. There are now national programs in 26 countries where the disease is endemic, and they are working in concert with NGOs, foundations, corporations, and the World Health Organization. One extraordinary example of the positive outcome of such a comprehensive, collaborative effort is that of Morocco. Blinding trachoma, which was a risk to 1.5 million people in Morocco just five years ago, will have been completely eliminated in the country by 2005—the most rapid ever single-country elimination program. As part of its $20 million initiative to prevent blindness due to trachoma, the Conrad N. Hilton Foundation is pleased to have provided funding in support of Helen Keller Worldwide's interventions in Morocco, choosing to focus on behavioral and environmental changes necessary for long-term elimination.

One of the most effective long-term solutions to preventing trachoma, as well as many other diseases and health problems, is giving people access to clean water along with education in proper hygiene and sanitation. Towards that end, the Conrad N. Hilton Foundation in 2002 launched the West Africa Water Initiative, a $40 million effort ($17 million of it from the Hilton Foundation) involving a collaboration of nonprofits, the U.S. Agency for International Development, foundations, individuals, and corporations. Working in the West African countries of Ghana, Mali, and Niger, the initiative will have as its goal to provide a minimum of 825 water wells, 100 alternative water sources, and more than 9,000 latrines among the three countries, benefiting half a million people.

Q: What can the tourism industry contribute to the solution?

A: Having worked at Hilton Hotels, I am aware of the enormous amount of resources that is consumed daily by hotels (electricity, natural gas, water, and the like). The Doubletree Hotel, part of the Hilton Hotels chain, located in Rohnert Park (Northern California), uses "gray water" from the city for irrigation, has cut energy use by changing lighting, and provides guests the option of not getting fresh sheets and towels every day. Through these efforts the hotel has been able to save money and be more environmentally responsible. Another example is Scandic Hotels, a division of Hilton International that has numerous hotel properties in northern Europe. These hotels have reduced operating costs while conserving resources. In fact, many guests decide to stay at the hotels because of their cutting-edge reputation and environmentally friendly practices.

Q: What can each of us do in order to conserve and protect the quality of water in our homes?

A: In our previous home in Malibu we used gray water—from showers, sinks, and laundry—to water the landscape. In addition, rainwater was collected from the roof and deck and channeled into a large tank for landscape watering. Our four acres were planted with trees and shrubs native to California and required far less water than the typical California garden. Just being mindful of how much water we use in our homes each day can make a difference in reducing our water consumption.

Q: What is the most important thing you believe we should all know with regard to water on Earth?

A: Clean water is essential for all life. As a consequence of the lack of access to safe drinking water and adequate sanitation, millions of people die every year of water-related diseases—mostly children, and mostly preventable deaths. The provision of clean water and adequate sanitation to those communities that lack these two essential necessities, both of which we take for granted in America, can save literally millions of lives each year!

SCIENTISTS ESTIMATE THERE ARE OVER ONE BILLION CUBIC
KILOMETERS OF WATER ON EARTH—ONE CUBIC KILOMETER
OF WATER WOULD FILL 300 OLYMPIC-SIZED SWIMMING POOLS

DR. KLAUS TOEPFER

EXECUTIVE DIRECTOR, UNITED NATIONS ENVIRONMENT PROGRAMME

Q: What do you think is the most unbearable thing happening to our blue planet?

A: Arguably, the freshwater crisis is the most urgent and serious problem. Pollution and related waterborne diseases are killing millions of people every year while severely degrading the aquatic environment in some parts of the world. In addition, water resources are being used faster than they are replenished in many areas. The disappearance of the Aral Sea is a classic example of this, as is the groundwater depletion in the Middle East. Some statistics highlight the severity of the fresh-water problem:

• Worldwide, about two-thirds of the population in 2025 are likely to be subject to moderate to high levels of water stress.

• Currently, about 20% of the world's population lack access to safe drinking water and 50% lack adequate sanitation.

• Worldwide, 2.1 million people die every year from diarrhoeal diseases (such as cholera and dysentery) caused by contaminated water.

• Polluted water affects the health of 1.2 billion people every year and contributes to the deaths of 15 million children under five every year.

• Vector-borne diseases, such as malaria, kill another 1.5 million to 2.7 million people per year, with inadequate water management a key cause of such diseases.

Q: Is it a viable option to export water from a water-rich country like Canada to solve the problems of countries lacking water, such as those in the Middle East or Africa?

A: It is technically viable, but a number of issues have not been sufficiently addressed. For example, could sufficient quantities of water be transported to make a difference—especially where there are no existing pipelines to transport water from ships to where it is most needed? What would the environmental implications be in the country supplying the water? Is it the most economic option?

Q: Has the international community been effective in tackling water problems?

A: It has to be said that the international community has not tackled water problems sufficiently. The statistics, as indicated above, bear this out. The international community recognises that the freshwater crisis is a key priority. That is why the World Summit on Sustainable Development (WSSD) and the Millennium Development Goals (MDG) have set critical targets in relation to freshwater:

• Halve, by the year 2015, the proportion of people without access to safe drinking water (reaffirmation of MDG).

• Halve, by 2015, the proportion of people who do not have access to basic sanitation.

• Develop integrated water resources management and water efficiency plans by 2005.

The organisation I'm involved with, the United Nations Environment Programme (UNEP), is primarily an environmental assessment and environmental policy advisory agency; thus it does not fund water infrastructure projects. The organisation assesses the extent and causes of water-related environmental problems and provides advice on how to fix these problems. UNEP, for example, offers advice on Integrated Water Resources Management (IWRM), the management of shared water resources, and water policy reform. UNEP also brings together countries and stakeholders to encourage a more coordinated approach to addressing water problems.

UNEP widely circulates its advice so that governments and water consumers can use water in an environmentally sustainable manner. This guidance includes information about environmentally sustainable techniques and technologies, such as rainwater harvesting, which is being practised in some areas.

Q: What are some of the solutions to the water crisis?

A: There needs to be a combination of water policy and management reform, capacity building, and increased financial resources. Water policy and management should have environmentally sustainable water use as their core objective. Tools such as IWRM are well proven and highlight that the key issue is implementation of agreed-upon actions, using well-tested tools.

Q: Is there anything else we need to know about water?

A: I think it is important to appreciate that environmentally sustainable freshwater use is vital for sustainable economic development, including poverty reduction. Too often the issue is seen as one of environment versus development. But environment for development is a more realistic concept.

Water is a key element of sustainable development because it is an essential component of life and income-generating activities. But for too long the environment has been seen as a competing user. However, this view of the environment as a competitor misses the critical point that the environment is fundamental to sustainable development. If water is used unsustainably, less of it is available to meet the needs of people. More specifically, if water is used consistently at a higher rate than it is replenished, or if it is polluted, thus restricted in use, then there are direct economic and social costs. The Aral Sea catastrophe is perhaps the best-known example of such economic cost.

Not only is sustainable water use a pillar of sustainable development, but, if appropriately managed, it could and should be a vital contributor to poverty reduction. The sustainable use of water provides economic benefits—by generating income, such as the growing of food, and good health. Conversely, unsustainable water use imposes costs through health problems and reduced production. While there is much focus on the costs of environmental protection, there is not enough focus on the costs of using the environment and water unsustainably. This is partly because these costs are often borne by those who have the least say—the poor.

Sustainable water use and sound water management produce reliable revenue flows, which can in turn be used to improve water supply to poor people and help all water users use water more efficiently through investment in appropriate end use technologies. Inefficient water management contributes directly to poverty. For example, in many cities water losses are 40% or more of total water supply! Conversely, water utility efficiency improvements would contribute directly to improving the environmental sustainability of water use and reducing poverty.

THERE ARE MORE THAN 6,000 OIL TANKERS
ROAMING THE SEAS EACH DAY, MANY OF THEM
IN A DANGEROUS STATE OF DISREPAIR

DR. MASARU EMOTO
PRESIDENT, I.H.M. COMPANY, LTD.

Q: Your photographs of water crystals indicate that thoughts and feelings affect their physical shape. Does this suggest there is a spiritual dimension to water?

A: Yes, I think so. My research of many years shows that the consciousness of people has a great impact on the quality of water. Water is the mirror that reflects the hado ("vibration" in Japanese) of its surroundings in the physical world. And I think that water has the same property in higher dimensions.

Q: How does human consciousness affect water? Do war and prayer affect water?

A: Water can catch and memorize vibration, however subtle it may be. And I think that human consciousness is a vibration as well. For this reason, I am sure that all vibrations, whether generated by war or by prayer, will affect water.

I have a number of practical examples. One instance occurred on January 17, 1991. I was measuring the hado of tap water at my office during that period using a machine called an MRA (Magnetic Resonance Analyser). We measure hado as a value ranging between +21 (the best) and -21 (the worst). Usually, when we measure Tokyo tap water, its hado values of such metal toxins as mercury, lead, and aluminium are between 0 and -6. But I found that these values had suddenly dropped to -13 to -19 on that morning. That was the day the Gulf war started.

Another example was recorded on July 25, 1999. Lake Biwa is the largest lake in Japan, and early that morning 350 people gathered by its shore and intoned a special prayer to bring harmony to its waters. The nasty, notorious smell from this very polluted lake, which had emanated from it every summer in previous years, was not reported at all during that summer. I could say that we were able to change the water metaphysically.

Furthermore, I have observed many occasions in various places around the world on which the shapes of water crystals changed into more beautiful and harmonious ones by our sending thoughts and feelings of love and thanks to water.

Q: What does a polluted water crystal look like?

A: In polluted water, you would not be able to observe a very beautiful, hexagonal water crystal shape. I think that the crystal is a visualization of the vibration held in the water. Vibration is the source of all existence. It is also the source of energy. Energy has two different aspects: destructive and creative. I think that the beauty or the ugliness of a water crystal indicates different aspects of energy.

Q: Where did the most beautiful water crystal you have ever found come from? And the ugliest?

A: The most beautiful crystal we observed was when we utilized a label that was typed with the words "love and thanks." We placed the label on a glass container with distilled water in it for 24 hours and then studied the water crystals, which were beautiful.

On the other hand, I have seen many ugly crystals. They have been found in various bodies of waters, including some that were chemically treated or some that were exposed to words like "you fool" or "evil." Some of the worst examples were taken from a polluted river. Needless to say, there are a lot of chemical toxins in a polluted river. Therefore, its water contains destructive energy, which we could describe as anti-life. Such water forms only a dirty crystal.

Q: Considering that the mature human body is made up by some 70% of water, do external events affect the water in our bodies?

A: As I said before, the origin of all life phenomena is hado—that is, vibration. As it happens, when you strike two tuning forks, a vibration resonates with, and is amplified by, another vibration when they have the same frequency. Similarly, if the water in your body has a good vibration, it will resonate only with a good vibration. Its energy will be amplified and influenced to a better direction by good energies radiating from the environment. When the vibration of your body is bad, it resonates with a bad vibration radiated from outside your body. It is also amplified and influenced in a bad way.

Q: What water is the safest to drink?

A: Of course, there are still wonderful natural waters, but unless we go to some countryside, it would be very difficult for us to find them. Therefore, the safest drinking water that I would recommend for people who live in an urban area is distilled water. Vibrationally speaking, it is the cleanest water.

Q: What is the single most important action we can take to positively affect the state of our planet's waters?

A: As I mentioned before, the most beautiful crystal I've seen was created when we used a label with the words "love and thanks" for 24 hours. Therefore, the most important action that we can take is to send our sincere love and thanks to all the water on the planet. On the basis of this idea, we started the Project of Love and Thanks to Water in July 2002. With it, we are proposing to send our love and thanks to water on July 25 every year simultaneously all over the world. We are sure that this action will change the quality of water on this planet.

Q: Do you have any other thoughts on the subject of water?

A: Water is ourselves. Life could not be born without water. And it is reported by NASA and other institutions that water has been coming from outer space to this planet in the form of countless numbers of huge ice blocks. Therefore, I think that we ourselves came from the universe and that water has been circulating through the universe, probably changing forms. This means that we will also change our forms and circulate through the universe. I think it is important for us to have this kind of universal view about ourselves.

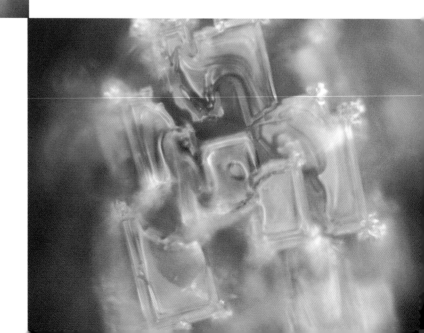

THE SHAPE OF WATER CRYSTALS
CHANGES WHEN EXPOSED
TO DIFFERENT SOUNDS

IN THE 110 COUNTRIES WHERE REEFS ARE FOUND,
30% HAVE PERISHED AND ANOTHER 30%
ARE AT RISK OF BECOMING SERIOUSLY DEPLETED

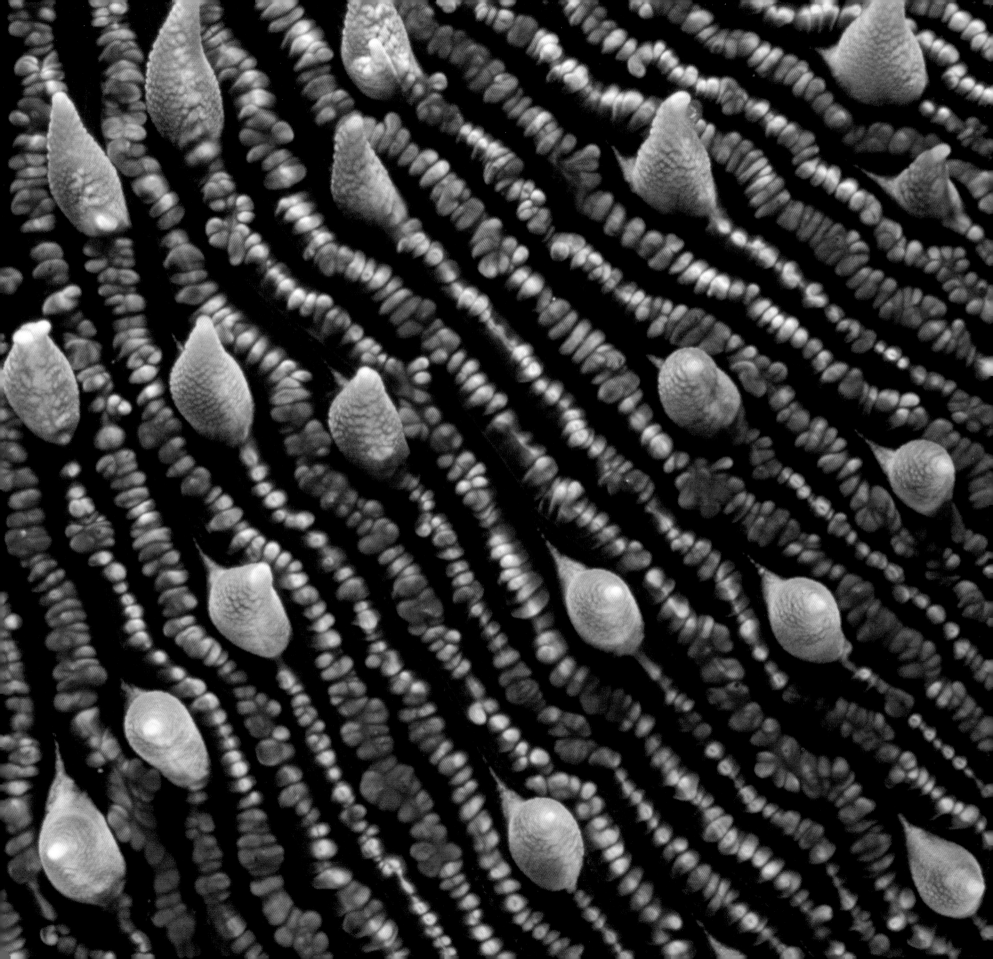

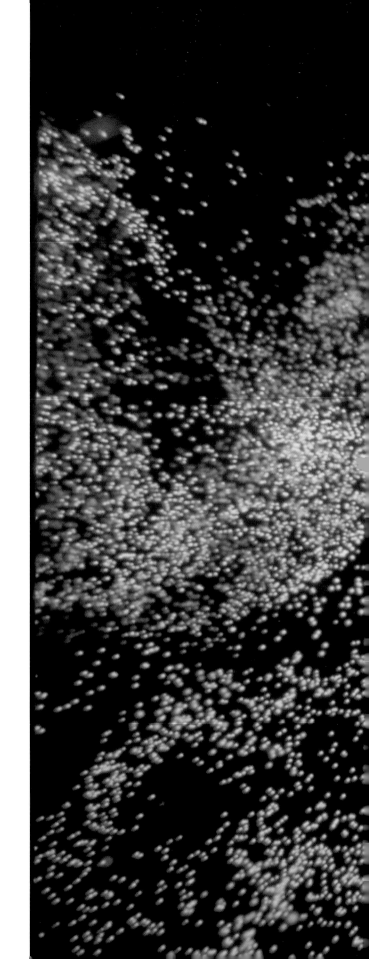

RICHARD SEARS
FOUNDER, MINGAN ISLAND CETACEAN STUDY

Q: What is it like to encounter a blue whale? This is a creature that averages 75 to 85 feet (27 to 30 meters) in length and is the largest mammal that has ever lived on Earth.

A: The slow, powerful motion of a blue whale coming to and through the surface never fails to amaze me. It's the same with a sudden and explosive 30-foot fountain from a spout, the resonance of that sound, and the mass of the whale's shoulders, head, and back slipping easily from water to air and then down again. And unless you've seen it, it's hard to convey the vision of several blue whale spouts hanging in crisp columns in still air; the power and speed of a pair or trio of blue whales racing, projecting half their bodies through the surface in great spumes of white spray; or a blue whale lunging high above the water line to feed, with its mouth wide open and forming a temporary 20-foot-high cave to gulp tons of water and krill.

But the real place to see blue whales is underwater, where they live. Beneath the surface there is direct intimacy with the size, grace, and fluidity of their form and movement.

Q: You have sailed many of the world's oceans over the past 29 years in search of the last remaining blue whales. What is their status?

A: Globally, their numbers probably peaked at 225,000 to 275,000; however, by the time of their protection in 1966, the blue whale population may have been reduced to 4,000 to 12,000. We hope that that figure is conservative and that there are more.

Q: Why are whales endangered? Does pollution play a role?

A: They are predominantly endangered because of the whaling that took place industrially up until the late 1950s. Some species, such as the minke, are still hunted by man today. Currently, one of the main concerns is how whales are being affected by persistent toxic pollutants. With great regularity, man produces new industrial chemical compounds that eventually find their way into the oceans. Waterborne pollutants are not an obvious, visible danger for whales to avoid, and so when they come into settled coastal areas to feed, their chances of coming into contact with some of man's less than noble products are pretty high. These pollutants can cause reproductive problems as well as cancerous lesions. And part of the problem is the time and cost it takes to determine the effect that pollutants have on mammalian systems.

In a more direct manner, high-shipping-traffic is taking its toll on the whale population. In this increasingly industrialized world, whales suffer deep wounds and casualties owing to collisions with ships. Vessels are abundant, and their object is to speed industrial goods and consumer products around the globe as quickly as possible. At least 15% of the blue whales in the St. Lawrence River in eastern Canada carry scars that can be attributed to ship strikes. Increased shipping also means more oil spill pollution, particularly from vessels in poor condition.

Q: In your view, are things getting better or are they getting worse for the planet's water ecosystems?

A: From the part of the world I know best, it would seem that humans are starting to get the right idea and are slowly turning the tide of abusive practices born of industrial and consumer greed. The waters of the St. Lawrence River in Canada, for

178

example, are getting a bit cleaner. We are, however, far from where we need to be, and reaching that place may take generations. We need to be increasingly vigilant and avoid complacency, particularly when we think that we have done enough because things appear superficially better.

Q: What can each one of us do to make things better?

A: Use water wisely; do not waste or taint it, whether on land or in the oceans. Treat and recycle wastewater in all communities. Strive to change injudicious public attitudes and influence the change of ineffective government policy.

Q: What role do you consider scientific research to have in determining the future course of water issues?

A: Continued research is necessary in all aspects of water use, including the ecology of freshwater and saltwater wetlands and in estuarine and oceanic systems. But science will not have the impact it can and should have if there is no confluence with education. We must also teach people how essential water is to all life on the planet. The research/education interface is vital to instruct humans how to make sound, judicious, and responsible use of water.

Q: Are you hopeful that human beings will someday learn to fully respect natural ecosystems and to live in harmony within them?

A: It will take a great deal of education and a conscious move away from the present, incompatible manner of acting economically first. We must learn to recognize the value of natural resources and try to better integrate sound ecological behavior into economic processes. We must temper injudicious economic development, uncontrolled industrial expansion, and consumption. We have to incorporate ecological and resource concerns into GNP thinking and economic projections at every level of community, be it county, province, state, nation, or continent.

Humans seem to be capable of anything. And the time is ripe to combine economic and ecologically sound creative thinking. If the essential global need to conserve really comes of age and we clearly recognize how vital it is to work together and not against each other and within natural systems, then, yes, we can live in harmony.

Q: What would you like everyone to know about water?

A: First and most important, it is life, pure and simple. When used respectfully by man, water can supply clean sources of energy and help feed the world. Water can also be a valuable indicator of how we affect the planet, by its quality, color, and clarity, but it can do even more than that. Water offers beauty in myriad ways throughout nature: oceans and ponds, trickles and waterfalls, streams and rivers can all come together with wind or currents to form a multitude of textures and shapes. Then, paired with light, water gives us countless strains of color, revealing endless faces. In man-made settings, water can be combined with natural or artificial light and sounds and sculptured materials, adding vitality in some spaces and creating calm in others.

Water is cleansing, therapeutic for body and mind, and vital to our survival. Yet it is the most abused substance on the planet.

THE EUPHRATES RIVER IS THE SOURCE
OF SIGNIFICANT POLITICAL TENSION—
TURKEY, SYRIA, AND IRAQ
ALL COMPETE FOR ITS WATERS TO IRRIGATE
AND GENERATE HYDROELECTRIC POWER

Mikhail Gorbachev, Russia (page 24)

Mikhail Gorbachev was the head of the Soviet Union from 1985 to 1991. Since 1992, he has been president of the International Foundation for Socio-Economic and Political Studies (The Gorbachev Foundation) and president of Green Cross International. He is the recipient of the Nobel Peace Prize (1990), the Orders of Lenin, the Red Banner of Labour, and the Badge of Honour. He is author of many books, the most recent being *On My Country and the World* (1999). <www.greencrossinternational.net>

Steven M. Hilton, U.S.A. (page 142)

As president of the Conrad N. Hilton Foundation, Steven Hilton carries on a family legacy that began with his grandfather, Conrad Hilton, the late hotel entrepreneur and founder of the foundation that bears his name. Steven joined the Foundation in 1983 and was named vice president in charge of programs in 1989. In this capacity, he directed the Foundation's grantmaking activities, with primary oversight of programs for the multi-handicapped blind, mentally ill homeless, and international water development. <www.hiltonfoundation.org>

Ryan Hreljac, Canada (page 106)

Ryan Hreljac is the founder of the Ryan's Well Foundation. Ryan's Well raises funds for water and sanitation projects in developing countries and encourages people everywhere to make a difference in the world. Ryan Hreljac, now 12, has helped to raise hundreds of thousands of dollars since he was six years old. Ryan has received many awards for his international development work, including the Canadian Peace Award and the Meritorious Service Medal from Canada's governor general. <www.ryanswell.ca>

Robert F. Kennedy, Jr., U.S.A. (page 56)

Mr. Kennedy serves as senior attorney for the Natural Resources Defense Council, chief prosecuting attorney for the Hudson Riverkeeper, and president of the Waterkeeper Alliance. He is also a clinical professor and supervising attorney at the Pace Environmental Litigation Clinic at Pace University School of Law in New York. The New York City watershed agreement, which he negotiated, is regarded as an international model in stakeholder consensus negotiations and sustainable development. <www.waterkeeper.org>

Richard M. Linnehan, U.S.A. (page 66)

NASA selected Dr. Linnehan to be a mission specialist in the United States Astronaut Corps in 1992. Prior to this, he served as chief clinical veterinarian for the U.S. Navy's Marine Mammal Program. A veteran of three space flights, Dr. Linnehan has logged more than 43 days in space, including three EVAs (space walks) totaling 21 hours and nine minutes. He is a member of the International Association of Aquatic Animal Medicine and the Association of Space Explorers, among other groups. <www.nasa.gov>

Richard Sears, U.S.A./France (page 178)

Richard Sears is founder and president of Mingan Island Cetacean Study, a research group dedicated to ecological studies of marine mammals. He established the first long-term studies of blue whales in both the North Atlantic and northeast Pacific oceans. He has studied blue whales in eastern Canada, Iceland, West Greenland, the Azores, the Antarctic, and the Sea of Cortez, Mexico. In 2002 his research led to the recognition of endangered status for the blue whale in Canadian waters. <www.rorqual.com>

Klaus Toepfer, Germany (page 156)

Dr. Toepfer is the executive director of the United Nations Environment Programme (UNEP). As minister of the environment in Germany, he introduced many ground-breaking environmental laws. He is known internationally for his commitment to sustainable development and for fighting for the cause of the developing world. Dr. Toepfer believes that environmental policy is the peace policy of the future and that social market economics coupled with wise environmental stewardship can improve the lives of all. <www.unep.org>

FACT REFERENCES

5   Environment Canada, <http://www.ec.gc.ca/water/en/e_quickfacts.htm>, viewed 25 July 2003.

18   Martineau, Daniel, *Diseases and Causes of Death of Beluga from the St Lawrence Estuary* (Quebec, Canada: Université de Montréal, May 2000), <http://205.236.172.1/ffstockrep/index_an.html>, viewed 1 July 2003.

32   The Aral Sea Homepage, <http://www.dfd.dlr.de/app/land/aralsee/back_info.html>, viewed 28 July 2003.

34   American University, *Chile Nitrates Exports*, <http://www.american.edu/TED/NITRATE.HTM>, viewed 25 July 2003.

35   Environment Canada, <http://www.ec.gc.ca/water/en/e_quickfacts.htm>, viewed 25 July 2003.

36   Environmental Information Exchange, <http://www.brookes.ac.uk/eie/oil.htm>, viewed 31 July 2003.

38   Pew Oceans Commission, <http://www.pewoceans.org/oceans/oceans_pollution.asp>, viewed 1 July 2003.

45   UNICEF, <http://www.unicef.org/specialsession/press/fast facts.htm>, viewed 1 July 2003.

54   World Water Council, <http://www.worldwatercouncil.org/Vision/6902B03438178538C125683A004BE974.htm>, viewed 1 July 2003.

59   Natural Resources Defense Council, *Testing the Waters 2002: A Guide to Water Quality at Vacation Beaches* (Washington, D.C.: NRDC, 2002): ex. summary.

64   IUCN Media Briefs, *Water & Wetlands*, <http://www.iucn.org/news/mbwater.pdf>, viewed 20 June 2003.

87   Pew Oceans Commission, *Fact Sheet: Cleaning Coastal Waters*, <http://www.pewoceans.org/oceans/oceans_pollution.asp>, viewed 1 July 2003.

88   Environmental Concern Inc., <http://www.wetland.org/educ_wet_func.htm>, viewed 1 July 2003.

99   The Carter Center, <http://www.cartercenter.org/healthprograms/showdoc.asp?programID=1&submenu=healthprograms>, viewed 20 June 2003.

100   UNEP, *World Water Day 1999*, <http://www.worldwaterday.org/1999/press.html>, viewed 1 July 2003.

103   UNESCO, <http://www.unesco.org/water/wwap/facts_figures/basic_needs.shtml>, viewed 20 June 2003.

135   United Nations Environment Programme, *Global Environment Outlook 2000* (London: Earthscan Publications, 1999).

137   Larsen, Janet, "Irrigated Area Raises." *Vital Signs 2002*. Publications of the Worldwatch Institute (New York: W. W. Norton & Company, 2002): 34.

139   Environment Canada, <http://www.ec.gc.ca/water/en/e_quickfacts.htm>, viewed 25 July 2003 & M. Catley-Carlson interview.

150   Environment Canada, <www.ec.gc.ca/water/en/nature/prop/e_here.htm>, viewed 25 July 2003.

162   WWF, <http://www.panda.org/news_facts/crisis/spain_oil_spill/index.cfm>, viewed 28 July 2003.

168   Emoto, Masaru, *Messages from Water* (Tokyo: HADO Kyoikusha Co., Ltd., 2002).

171   IUCN Media Briefs, *Ocean Blues*, <http://www.iucn.org/news/mbocean.pdf>, viewed 20 June 2003

195   Suite 101.com, <http://www.suite101.com/article.cfm/middle_east/28688>, viewed 28 July 2003.

203   Gleick, Peter H., *The World's Water: The Biennial Report of Freshwater Resources 2002-2003* (Washington: Island Press, 2002): 210.

CREDITS & ACKNOWLEDGEMENTS

Water Culture is a SKeGROUP project
in partnership with
Jean-Michel Cousteau's Ocean Futures Society

Credits
Editors Marisha Shibuya & Francesca Sorrenti & Gigi
Designers The Fold, www.thefold.net
Text editor David E. Cashion
Copy-editor Judith Sonntag
Proof-reader Navorn Johnson
Project assistant Christine Lozier

Ocean Futures Society
Editor Pam Stacey
Executive Vice President Charles Vinick

Acknowledgments
To the photographers whose art illuminates these pages
and who all graciously and enthusiastically jumped into
this endeavor with us, we are so deeply indebted.

To the interviewees whose groundbreaking knowledge
and wisdom enrich the book with powerful ideas,
your work, courage, and dedication provides enduring
inspiration, for which we remain deeply appreciative.

Magnum Photos (www.magnumphotos.com), is a
photographic co-operative of great diversity and
distinction owned by its photographer-members. With
powerful individual vision, Magnum photographers
chronicle the world and interpret its peoples, events,
issues, and personalities.

Corbis (www.corbis.com), founded by Bill Gates
in 1989, is the world's preeminent visual solutions
provider—licensing images seen by millions of people
daily in advertising, books, newspapers, magazines,
on TV, and in films.

Big Magazine (www.bigmagazine.com) for their
help in photography research.
Andrew Gursky's photograph courtesy of Matthew
Marks Gallery, New York.

Bill Henson, Anna Zahalka's photographs courtesy
of Roslyn Oxley9 Gallery, Sydney.

Sponsorship
Without their contributions, this project would never have
seen the light of day, and we are deeply indebted to the
following people and institutions for their generosity:
• United Nations Environment Programme
• Jarret Schecter
• International Development Research Centre
  The IDRC is a public corporation created by the
  Parliament of Canada in 1970 to help developing
  countries use science and technology to find
  practical, long-term solutions to the social, economic,
  and environmental problems they face. Support is
  directed toward developing an indigenous research
  capacity to sustain policies and technologies
  developing countries need to build healthier,
  more equitable, and more prosperous societies.

Masaru Emoto's Team for Messages from Water:
Jun Futamura, Kazuki Hamano, Kazunari Ishibashi,
Masaya Sato

When we set on board this project, many people
heeded to our calls for help, and we thank them from
the bottom of our hearts:
Adnan Amin, Louis Aubin, Kelly Blevins, Hieu Tom Boui,
William J. Cosgrove, Charlotte Cotton, Tim Dottridge,
Jacob Duer, Lindsay Evans, Éric Falt, Lucia Fernandez,
Mary Frey, Michele Glisson, Jennifer Hayes, Brian
Hetherington, Hreljac family, Karin Hulshof, Gianni
Jacklone, Markus Jans, Maaike Jansen, Zeke Johnson,
Marcelo Juneman, Haley Mack, Markus Kiersztan, Petra
Langhammer, Ricky Lee, Alexander Likhotal, David
Maloney, John Marchant, Sarah Marusek, Marcel
Massé, Rohinton Medhora, Sheryl Mendez, Yasuyuki
Nemoto, Valentina Petrelli, Mary Beth Postman, Claire
Powell, Ruby Russell, Eri Satoh, Hiro Shibuya, Jim
Sniffen, Heather Sommerfield, Jeanette Song'e, Amy
Spindler, Max Stamper, David Strettel, Steve Sutton,
Vanessa Tobin, Lesa Wang, Jessica Warner, Neville
Wakefield, Chantal Weber, Oliver Wood; all the
photographers' agents, managers, and assistants;
the staff at Ocean Futures Society, Sarah Ettman-
Sterner, Barbara Lapiana, Carrie Vonderhaar; the staff
at Purple, Andrew Ferguson, Hally Logan, Caroline
Lynch, Gillian McVey; Fotolito, Art Partners,
Art & Commerce, MAP, and Unit Creative Management.

SKeGROUP (info@skegroup.com)
see, know, & evolve—A unique group (founded by
Francesca Sorrenti and Marisha Shibuya) that brings
about awareness to environmental, social, and artistic
issues. SKe puts visual art to the service of knowledge
and education, bringing them to life through creative
art and literary expression. SKe unites cutting edge
photographers, illustrators, designers, prominent
experts, and publishers while researching topics
that need awareness in today's world.

Francesca Sorrenti, co-founder of SKeGROUP, has
been involved in the arts for many years from fashion
designing to advertising-creative director for a large
corporation. She then moved on to a ten-year career in
photography working for many well-known publications
worldwide. She was curator of Photoart, a photography
exhibition, and co-editor of the companion special
edition book Toma, benefiting the Cooley's anemia
Foundation, and she has worked with youths in drug
awareness projects within the fashion industry.
Francesca has edited photography books pertaining
to social and environmental issues.

Marisha Shibuya has worked as an environmental
consultant for private, public, and not-for-profit
businesses and international organizations in Canada,
the U.S.A., Europe, Africa, Central America, and Asia.
She has written, researched, and produced numerous
scientific articles and educational publications. She is
co-author of the 2002 "Children in the New Millennium"
report on children's environmental health, published
by the United Nations. Marisha, originator of the Water
Culture concept, is co-founder of the SKeGROUP.

Ocean Futures Society (www.oceanfutures.org)
OFS was founded by Jean-Michel Cousteau. It is
dedicated to the mission of exploring our global ocean,
inspiring and educating people to act responsibly
for its protection, documenting the critical connection
between humanity and nature, and celebrating
the ocean's vital importance to the survival of life
on our planet.

Pamela Stacey has been a writer and editor for Jean-
Michel Cousteau in a variety of magazines, book series
and film projects and is director of publications
at Ocean Futures Society.

Charles Vinick has worked with Jean-Michel Cousteau
for more than 25 years developing and directing
projects. He is executive vice-president of Ocean
Futures Society.

Published in Great Britain in 2003
by Trolley Ltd Unit 5
London E2 8HN, UK
Distributed by Phaidon Press

10 9 8 7 6 5 4 3 2 1

A catalogue record for this book is available
from the British Library

ISBN 1-904563-09-0

Design by The Fold
Editing by red@zioni
Printed in Italy by Soso Industrie Grafiche S.p.A.

TABLE OF CONTENTS